Proceedings of the Large Jail Network Meeting
Aurora, Colorado
September 28–30, 2014

U.S. Department of Justice
National Institute of Corrections

Michael P. Jackson
Correctional Program Specialist
Large Jail Network Program Coordinator

October 10, 2014

Connie Clem
Meeting Recorder
Clem Information Strategies
Longmont, Colorado

About the Large Jail Network

The National Institute of Corrections (NIC) established the Large Jail Network (LJN) in 1989 as a connection point for administrators of jails and jail systems housing 1,000 or more inmates. The network was launched with 67 member agencies and convened at its first meeting in 1990. Participants meet twice yearly, in the spring and fall.

The contact for information about the Large Jail Network is Mike Jackson, Correctional Program Specialist, NIC Jails Division, Washington, D.C., (800) 995-6423, ext. 69565, or *mpjackson@bop.gov*.

NIC provides a private web site for the LJN, where members can access presentation files from this and earlier LJN meetings as well as share other materials throughout the year. A member forum facilitates a day-to-day dialogue on issues facing large jails and strategies for responding to them. Current and prospective members can access the site at *http://community.nicic.org/forums*.

Purpose

The NIC Jails Division networks' mission is to promote and provide a vehicle for the free and open exchange of ideas and information and innovation among network members. In addition, NIC networks reinforce the assumption that knowledge can be transferred from one jurisdiction or agency to another, and this knowledge can serve as a stimulus for the development of effective approaches to address similar problems or opportunities.

Our belief is that, collectively, network members are likely to have developed successful strategies for meeting challenges that arise. As a group, network members are an available resource to each other. The network provides a systematic way for information to be shared, which not only benefits the network member, but also those they serve and represent – the local government, state, community, staff, and inmate.

LJN Goals

➢ To explore issues facing jail systems from the perspective of network members with administrative responsibility.

➢ To discuss strategies and resources for dealing successfully with these issues.

➢ To discuss potential methods by which NIC can facilitate the development of programs or the transfer of existing knowledge or technology.

➢ To develop and improve communication among network members.

➢ To seek new and creative ways to identify and meet the needs of network members.

CONTENTS

About This Meeting 1

Legal Issues in Today's Jails: Avoiding Civil Liability 2
    Carrie Hill, Esq., Maple Grove, Minnesota

Domestic Threats to Jail Security 8
    Part 1. Countering Prisoner Radicalization in the Federal Bureau of Prisons 8
    Jeff Woodworth, U.S. Bureau of Prisons
    Part 2. Sovereign Citizens 10
    Steve Cope, U.S. Bureau of Prisons, Counterterrorism Unit

Prison Rape Elimination Act—Lessons Learned from Early Audits 12
    Part 1. PREA: The Riverside Regional Jail Authority Experience 12
    Jeffery Newton, Riverside Regional Jail, Virginia
    Part 2. Surviving the PREA Audit 15
    Marilyn Chandler Ford, Volusia County, Florida

Health Care Reform + Inmate Medical Care = Reduced Costs? 17
    Part 1. The Affordable Care Act: Continuity of Care 17
    Richelle Anhalt, Dane County, Wisconsin
    Part 2. Affordable Care Act: Innovative Approaches 18
    Raul Banasco, Bexar County, Texas
    Part 3. Curbing the Rising Cost of Health Care 19
    Mark Bolton, Louisville Metro Corrections, Kentucky

Mental Health Models that Work 21

    Part 1. Restoration of Competency Program 21

        Gregory Garland, San Bernardino County, California

    Part 2. Mental Health Treatment...22

        Christopher Kneisley, Palm Beach County, Florida

    Part 3. Mental Health Management Unit...22

        Jared Schecter, Sedgwick County, Kansas

    Part 4. Mental Health Treatment and Community Re-entry 23

        Don Pinkard, Gwinnett County, Georgia

Jail Leader Longevity in Office 25

        Patrick Tighe, St. Lucie County, Florida

Open Forum 28

    Body Cameras 28

    Restricted Housing 28

    Scanning Drivers Licenses for Visitor Registry 29

    Scheduling Visitation 29

    Internal Affairs Investigator Training 29

    Preserving the Security of Facility Plans...29

    E-Cigarettes 29

    Kosher Kitchens...30

    Contract Monitors 30

    Part-Time Employees 30

    Immigration Holds..30

    Insurance for Community Service Participants 31

    Rotating Duty Post Assignments 31

    Arts Programs...31

    Funding for Religious Items 31

    Transgender Correctional Staff..32

    Suboxone 32

Professional Association Updates 33

    American Correctional Association News 33

        Ben Shelor, American Correctional Association, Alexandria, Virginia

    American Jail Association News 34

        Bob Kasabian, American Jail Association, Hagerstown, Maryland

    National Sheriffs' Association News 34

        Tim Albin, Tulsa County, Oklahoma

Future Meeting Topics 35

APPENDICES

Appendix A. LJN September 2014 Final Meeting Agenda

Appendix B. LJN September 2014 Participant List

Appendix C. Index of Past LJN Meeting Topics

ABOUT THIS MEETING

The September 2014 Large Jail Network meeting took place at the National Institute of Corrections, National Corrections Academy in Aurora, Colorado. There were 63 detention agency staff in attendance.

The meeting began with an informal dinner on Sunday, September 28, with an opening session and participant and guest introductions. Two days of presentations and discussion followed.

Guests and speakers at the meeting included:

➢ Carrie Hill, Esq., Maple Grove, Minnesota;

➢ Jeff Woodworth, U.S. Bureau of Prisons;

➢ Steve Cope, U.S. Bureau of Prisons, Counterterrorism Unit;

➢ Bob Kasabian, Executive Director, American Jail Association, Hagerstown, Maryland; and

➢ Ben Shelor, Assistant Director, Standards, Accreditation, and Professional Development, American Correctional Association, Alexandria, Virginia;

➢ Connie Clem, meeting recorder, Clem Information Strategies, Longmont, Colorado.

The agenda for the meeting is provided in Appendix A.

A list of LJN members in attendance and meeting guests appears in Appendix B.

An index of past topics covered at LJN meetings is provided in Appendix C.

PROGRAM SESSION: LEGAL ISSUES

LEGAL ISSUES IN TODAY'S JAILS: AVOIDING CIVIL LIABILITY

Presenter: Carrie Hill, Esq., Maple Grove, Minnesota

Carrie Hill shared key principles for running a safe jail and for positioning the jail for optimal legal defense in the event of a lawsuit. She also discussed lessons that can be applied from recent court decisions in the areas of supervisor liability, searches, and use of force to restore order.

Hill offered several perspectives on the legal aspects of running a jail.

➢ Hill prefers that jails not agree to settle their lawsuits. Doing so sets a precedent, it gives inmates something to talk about, but most importantly it can affect staff morale. If an agency is going to settle a lawsuit, it's important to tell the staff why. Did staff do their jobs correctly? Did something in the legal or operational environment change?

➢ The U.S. Supreme Court makes it clear that court decisions must give substantial deference to the agency, because the correctional agency knows the most about the business of running the jail. This is expressed in the four-part test from *Turner v. Safley*:

  1. Is there a valid, rational connection between the regulation or practice and the legitimate governmental interest put forward to justify it?
  2. Are there alternative means of exercising the basic right that remain available to the inmate?
  3. Will accommodating the asserted right have a reasonable or a disproportionate impact on officers and other inmates and on the allocation of prison resources?
  4. Does the agency have obvious, easy alternatives to achieve the same end, or is the regulation an exaggerated response?

  The Turner framework should be reflected in the agency's policies and procedures, its officer training, its report writing, and in its processes for after-incident review. The first prong is the most important: there must be a rational connection between policy and a legitimate governmental interest, such as safety, security, order, control, or discipline.

➢ After-incident reviews are a vital self-audit tool for jails to improve practice. Agencies should not limit their reviews to only their critical incidents. The details of any situation may be significant. Review of video evidence is valuable. What did staff do well, what could be improved, what stands out? The review allows leaders to open a dialog with staff and address issues in training or policy. If mistakes were made, own them, move forward, and make changes if needed. Ideally the mistake is an isolated event, not part of a custom, policy, or practice. An agency that can demonstrate it does this self-prompted review and auditing can argue that it doesn't owe the plaintiffs even their attorney fees.

- ➤ Automated jail management system (JMS) reports can be adjusted so they are based more directly on the elements that the courts look for: the rationale for an action, the safety and security factors, etc.

- ➤ The report entered into the JMS should state a brief synopsis of the incident. Details should be included in supplemental documentation.

- ➤ Reports and reviews should document any aggravating and mitigating factors—in both the live incident response and in the agency's handling of it. This protects the agency and helps to explain the incident and response to other staff. An officer's years of service matter, for example. If a staff member who made a major error is not terminated, the documentation should state specifically why.

- ➤ *Sandin v. Conner* is a Supreme Court case that establishes that policies are guidelines, and sometimes staff must step outside of them to do their jobs appropriately. These actions do not violate policy, if the rationale substantiates them. Reporting and policy language should not refer to these actions as violations of policy.

- ➤ Agencies should modify their policy language to move away from the term, "suicide watch." The term "heightened watch" is more appropriate and reflects the objective criteria jails use when classifying inmates. Similarly, agencies should stop using the term "isolation" and instead refer to "restricted housing."

Supervisor Liability

Starr v. Baca, a 2011 case from the 9th Circuit Court of Appeals, addressed supervisors' personal liability. In this case, an inmate sued on the basis that he was stabbed after asking jail personnel for protection, but a door was left open, allowing an assault to occur. Plaintiffs' attorneys argued for the first time that a sheriff should be personally liable under the deliberate indifference standard.

Farmer v. Brennan defines the four-part test for deliberate indifference.

1. Is there a substantial risk of harm? Yes, it's a jail environment with inherent potential risks.

2. Did the jail staff have knowledge of the risk? Yes, Baca had direct knowledge of risk in the jail as well as access to U.S. Department of Justice reports on danger in the facility. He knew that inmates who have been in jail previously are likely to pose more danger to others and that the jail held gang members.

3. Did jail staff disregard the risk, despite their knowledge of the risk? This is the pivotal factor. It's irrelevant what a reasonable person might infer in a situation. The content of deputies' reports is critical. Did they have any reason to draw an inference that an assault might happen in this specific instance, on the basis of what they knew was going on in the housing unit? The presence of rival gang members per se is irrelevant if they normally conduct themselves appropriately. The true question is, on that specific day, was something going on between inmates that was ignored? Did the officer know of a specific risk but do nothing about it?

4. Did the conduct of jail staff cause harm? The inmate was injured. If the injury was caused or enabled by staff, the agency may discipline the officer, boost training, or take other steps.

The agency has a better position when it can show that an incident was an isolated event and does not reflect how officers were trained or supervised, nor does it reflect the custom, policy, or practice of the agency. Testing is useful because it documents that at that moment, a staff member knew a fact such as the difference between a pat and a strip search.

In a situation with observable excessive force, anyone can have "bystander liability." If a staff member sees or has knowledge of excessive force occurring, they must intervene. Otherwise plaintiffs can claim that the conduct is an accepted custom, policy, or practice.

Knowing about an issue and attempting to address it shows the agency was not indifferent. The agency should articulate its reasoning and either correct the situation immediately or continue to work toward correcting it.

One agency faced a lawsuit after an inmate suicide. The inmate submitted a medical visit request via a kiosk, writing that he needed to talk with someone about a problem. He was moved to a different unit and completed the suicide before medical personnel reached him. The inmate had been in the jail before and had mental health issues. At intake, he said he did not feel suicidal. Therefore staff could not reasonably infer he was a suicide risk and were not found deliberately indifferent.

Discussion

➢ Jail leadership should talk (at an appropriate level) with staff about an incident while the internal affairs review is under way and use the opportunity to emphasize the importance of good reporting. Openness dispels rumors. Complete the IA investigation even if the person resigns or retires and even if there will be a criminal investigation.

➢ Notice the little things that are happening. Is something blocking the view through a cell window? Is there trash out? Are you watching all your use of force videos, and/or is one person reviewing them for consistency? Do officers take a detainee's belt but allow him to keep his shoes and shoelaces? Do inmates empty their own pockets? After a use of force incident in booking, does someone clean up right away or preserve the evidence? Details that don't rise to a constitutional violation can undermine the agency's position later. If a pat search skips the waist region, the officer may say the supervisor never corrected her. In that case, ask the supervisor if she noticed the lapse and if so, did she intervene?

➢ If parts of the facility aren't on video surveillance, this is not a violation. But now that the agency knows it has a blind spot, what action is taken?

➢ Video evidence very likely protects staff and the agency. The agency's position is not necessarily weakened greatly if an officer remembers throwing three punches and the video shows there were actually seven. However, errors of this type are less likely when staff can see the video, either prior to writing the report or before the final version is submitted. Video evidence exists to provide the jail administration a complete and accurate story. However, it often shows only the incident itself, without the lead-up or the actions immediately following.

> Agencies should track data on the use of the Taser™. It's considered a successful use of force if the Taser™ is removed from the holster but not used. One agency has documented 500 deterrent uses and 50 incidents in which the trigger was squeezed.

> Staff may be held liable for attorney's fees when acting outside the scope of their employment. The settlement award itself may be small (for example, $1), but the attorney fees add up. This is one reason not to accept settlements.

> Providing inmates ample opportunity to grieve helps the agency resolve issues at the lowest possible level. Timelines should be generous. Issues can't be filed in federal court until they've been addressed through the grievance process and administrative remedies have been exhausted. Some states have their own version of the Prison Litigation Reform Act, which is beneficial for corrections agencies.

Participants viewed a video segment showing a less than professional use of force and critiqued the staff's performance for elements that could increase liability. This is a useful training exercise.

Inmate Searches

Strip searches are necessary to support legitimate government interests, such as contraband control, tattoo-based recognition of security threat group members, and the identification of medical issues. The agency's security interests must be balanced against the inmate's expectation of privacy. Safety comes first. Jails should conduct appropriate searches and get the inmates covered again.

Bell v. Wolfish defined a four-part test when looking at strip search policies:

1. The need for the search.

2. The intrusiveness of the search.

3. The person or persons who conduct the search.

4. Where the search is done.

Bell v. Wolfish also said agencies can strip-search arrestees before they are put into a general population unit. Only in arrestee status is reasonable suspicion/probable cause required before a strip search is permissible.

The manner and location of the search are the factors that most often lead to litigation. A decision tree is useful in intake to help anticipate issues such as who will conduct a strip search of a transgender detainee.

Staff must understand the differences between different types of searches, and they should be clearly defined in policy.

> A pat search involves physical touching of the exterior of the individual's clothing.

> A strip search involves the visual review of an individual's body. They must be conducted by a same-sex staff member in a location with privacy from other viewers, and they cannot

be videotaped. Jail policy does not need to distinguish between a strip search and a visual body cavity search.

> A body cavity search involves physical contact with the individual's body. If a digital body cavity search is needed, it should be performed by medical personnel.

> A forced clothing removal is not a strip search; it is a use of force incident. It can be performed by staff of any sex and may be videotaped.

Bell v. Wolfish made clear that jails can strip search detainees before they enter the general population. However, there are unaddressed issues in the law. The agency's ability to search inmates who are not necessarily going to general population is unclear, and the Court provided no definition of "general population." A working definition of general population could include any area of the facility where substantial contact with one or more other inmates is likely, including booking, general housing, administrative segregation, and the infirmary. If an inmate is not necessarily going to be housed in general population, appropriateness to search is less clear.

Body scanning technology is useful, particularly in booking, where most contraband is found. It is a less intrusive method for identifying contraband. If the agency finds contraband, this provides a rationale for further searching. A staff member of the same sex should view the scanned image if possible.

If an inmate makes it into booking with a weapon, this information can be passed along to law enforcement so that agency can improve its training on search techniques.

If a cell phone is found incident to a lawful arrest, the agency should get a warrant before accessing the phone contents. But if an inmate has a cell phone, this is a rule infraction that constitutes a risk of escape or other criminal dealings, so the jail can open it. An outside agency would need a warrant to do so. Similarly, if a cell phone is found on an on-duty staff member, the phone can be searched because it represents a policy breach. However, the agency likely should obtain a warrant first and/or provide for the staff member's counsel to be present.

Use of Force: Response to Resistance

Hudson v. McMillan identifies five elements that indicate the objective reasonableness of the use of force.

1. The threat perceived by a reasonable officer.

2. The need for use of force.

3. The amount of force used in relation to the need for force.

4. The effort(s) made to temper forceful response.

5. The extent of resulting injury.

Jail incident reports should articulate what threat was perceived. In exigent circumstances, officers must respond. The key is that they must make a good faith effort to restore order, not apply force willfully and sadistically with the intent to cause harm.

Response should be proportional. A "use of force continuum" is useful as a framework in training, but live events happen too quickly for analysis. The officer's report must say specifically what the inmate was doing throughout the incident, such as hitting the officer or pushing the officer off. This documents the need for continued force to contain the threat. Reports should indicate all efforts made to temper the use of force, such as verbal commands and escort holds. If there is an injury, the report should say that the inmate was referred for medical care but provide no further details.

One jail posted a sign stating that inmates who fail to reply with orders would be Tased. The jail was successfully sued when officers used the Taser™ on an inmate who refused to leave his bunk because he was suffering from back pain. The threat perceived was disproportionate to the force used.

Positional asphyxia is a risk in use of force incidents. Officers should be trained to get the inmate on his side as quickly as possible after the inmate is controlled.

Attorney Carrie Hill can be reached at *clsh@comcast.net* or 612-306-4831.

- - -

PROGRAM SESSION: DOMESTIC THREATS TO JAIL SECURITY

PART 1. COUNTERING PRISONER RADICALIZATION IN THE FEDERAL BUREAU OF PRISONS

Presenter: Jeff Woodworth, U.S. Bureau of Prisons representative, National Joint Terrorism Task Force

Correctional intelligence programs are focused on the identification and management of inmates who may pose a threat to facility security because of links to or sympathy with terrorist groups. They may be in corrections custody for reasons related or unrelated to their alleged offense or crime of conviction. They may be detained on minor charges. They may have extreme political or religious beliefs before entering the jail or may become radicalized while in custody. Once radicalized, these people are not likely to change their views. The Bureau of Prisons (BOP) is taking part in several initiatives aimed at limiting the risk they pose.

Which Inmates Pose a Threat?

Belief is not the issue; behavior is. Members of several internationally significant security threat groups are in BOP custody. Examples include Al Qaida, Al Shabaab, Hamas, Hizbollah, Laskar-E-Tayyiba, Taliban, the Tamil Tigers, and the United Forces of Columbia.

The BOP refers to Americans who become radicalized as homegrown violent extremists (HVEs). Some inmates in this category are members of U.S.-based organizations including the Earth Liberation Front, the Army of God, the Montana Freemen, the Aryan Nation, the Phineas Priesthood, and the Order. Others who pose a threat are loners. Recruitment and radicalization takes place through personal connections, online, and through magazines and other print material. Actions prompted by extreme religious and social beliefs may result in arrest and incarceration.

Some inmates hate the government and/or blame government for personal and social problems, including their own disenfranchisement. They don't accept responsibility for the crimes that put them in custody. People with this point of view may be more likely to become radicalized in custody. A related group is known as "sovereign citizens," whose extreme views include a refusal to pay taxes.

Radicalization can begin when a charismatic inmate makes contact with one who is receptive. As the recruit accepts the radical ideology, he or she can become indoctrinated and progressively more likely to become an active participant in criminal activity in the jail and beyond.

BOP Strategy

The BOP has an estimated 300 inmates who are known members of international terrorist organizations and about 100 inmates who are members of known domestic terrorist groups. About another 600 federal inmates are sovereign citizens. The most dangerous inmates are held at the BOP's administrative maximum security facility in Florence, Colorado, and two other locations.

BOP's counterterrorism unit (CTU) is tasked with identifying and validating all terrorist offenders in custody. Criteria aside from crime of conviction include content in presentence reports and/or a nexus or direct contact with a security threat group. The CTU shares information with all BOP facilities and community locations plus FBI's National Joint Terrorism Task Force (JTTF). Every JTTF location has a correctional intelligence coordinator.

Information can be shared in the FBI's Guardian program. It allows law enforcement agencies to share and access information such as telephone numbers, recordings, and emails without a subpoena.

What Jails Can Do

Jails should identify and manage inmates in their custody who may pose a potential terrorist threat.

- Monitor who an inmate is associating with and communicating with.

- Monitor inmates' mail for extremist publications. Titles to watch for may change. *Inspired* magazine and *Azan* are two to be aware of. Articles have addressed bomb-making and calls for violent jihad.

- Provide training to staff on what to look for as an indicator of suspicious activity.

- If someone (including a volunteer or contractor) wants to be added to an inmate's visiting list, be cautious if something doesn't seem right.

- Coordinate security procedures, such as running security checks on all volunteers and others coming into the facility.

- Make sure volunteers aren't bringing in inappropriate print materials.

- Watch for charismatic inmates who want to challenge or remove religious authorities.

- Pay attention to signals such as inmates going silent when a staff member enters a religious meeting.

- Scrutinize any requests or attempts to engage in military drill or martial arts training.

- Watch for signs that inmates are disparaging faith traditions other than their own.

- Be cautious about allowing inmates to act as leaders in religious services or other gatherings. Ensure that religious gatherings follow a script or observance guidelines, or make an audio or video recording of the meetings.

- When the jail houses an inmate of concern, notify the BOP and FBI. Participate in the FBI's Guardian program, which provides a system for reporting suspicious activity, and the Correctional Intelligence Initiative, the partnership between law enforcement and corrections created to fight against terrorism. Forge a relationship with the liaison officer at the nearest of the FBI's 56 field offices. Stay connected with the nearest Fusion Center. Ensure that the agency's intelligence supervisor is using the law enforcement officer enterprise portal.

PART 2. SOVEREIGN CITIZENS

Presenter: Steve Cope, U.S. Bureau of Prisons, Counterterrorism Unit

In July 2014, the National Consortium for the Study of Terrorism and Responses to Terrorism released the results of a survey of law enforcement professionals, in which they identified sovereign citizens as a top threat posed to communities. Sovereign citizens consider themselves to be in lawful rebellion against the federal government. They may be detained or convicted on various charges, such as tax fraud or tax defiance.

One way they pose a risk is their method of filing liens against correctional officials and staff members. The agency then needs to provide legal assistance to the staff to have the liens removed. Beyond this, some are moving away from paper terrorism and into acts of criminal violence, including armed incidents involving law enforcement. In a few incidents, representatives have come to prisons claiming to be marshals of a fourth branch of government and demanding the release of specific inmates.

Cope said there are two types of sovereign citizens. Some are new to the cause and are aiming to get financial benefits. The second type has a strong animosity toward government.

The rationale behind the sovereign citizen movement began to evolve with the Posse Comitatus revival in the 1970s. It claims that the sheriff is the highest law enforcement official in the country, that the federal government has no jurisdiction in the states, that only residents of the District of Columbia are U.S. citizens, among other views. Roger Elvick's "redemption theory" emerged during the Farm Aid era of U.S. economic uncertainty.

The National Liberty Alliance is one of the largest organizations of sovereign citizens and is claiming the right to convene common law grand juries. Various local organizations also exist. For example, the Republic of Texas has 40,000 members and has minted its own coins. The Little Shell Pembina Band of North America has a Native American connection and makes its own license plates.

Today, material is shared in YouTube videos and elsewhere. According to the movement, each American has a governmental identity and government trust account anchored by the social security number. Adherents seek to access these supposed trust account funds by filing a series of legal documents. These transactions establish a legal relationship between the actual person and their supposed paper/government equivalent.

Once the paper identity has been created, inmates can use it to file liens on correctional staff members' property, claiming damages for being unlawfully incarcerated, wrongful discipline, etc.

Cope gave an example: an officer who writes an inmate disciplinary report is said to be executing a contract with the inmate. The inmate will then start a private administrative process involving multiple self-executing notices. If they are ignored, the staff member's silence is considered to be acquiescence and the lien is filed.

BOP Response

The BOP has designated sovereign citizens as a security threat group. Currently more than 500 BOP inmates are identified as involved in the group, up from about 300 in 2010.

The BOP uses several methods to control their activities.

➤ The forms used in establishing the alternate identity or any legal or financial action connected with it are considered contraband.

➤ Inmates found to have mailed such documents are charged with using the U.S. Mail for an illegal purpose.

➤ Telephone access will be restricted to two, 15-minute phone calls per week. Visits also are limited.

➤ An act passed in 2007 makes it a crime punishable by 10 years in prison to file a false lien against a federal employee. Several states have enacted similar laws.

➤ The BOP provides guidance to its personnel on how to file against fraudulent financial instruments.

➤ LexisNexis can be searched for liens against corrections personnel. Because inmates can file liens in any state, it's necessary to check all jurisdictions.

Cope assists BOP personnel with issues and questions related to sovereign citizens, including inmate property, documents, and how to write incident reports. For more information and assistance, LJN members can contact Steve Cope at *scope@bop.gov* or 304-262-8322.

See also:

START website: *http://www.start.umd.edu/*

Carter, David, and Steve Chermak, Jeremy Carter, and Jack Drew. (2014.) "Understanding Law Enforcement Intelligence Processes," Report to the Office of University Programs, Science and Technology Directorate, U.S. Department of Homeland Security. College Park, MD: START, 2014. *http://www.start.umd.edu/publication/understanding-law-enforcement-intelligence-processes*

– – –

PROGRAM SESSION: PRISON RAPE ELIMINATION ACT— LESSONS LEARNED FROM EARLY AUDITS

PART 1. PREA: THE RIVERSIDE REGIONAL JAIL AUTHORITY EXPERIENCE

Presenter: Jeffery Newton, Superintendent, Riverside Regional Jail Authority, North Prince George, Virginia

Jeffery Newton observed that engaging the PREA audit process can trigger constructive evolution in a corrections agency. The Riverside Regional Jail (RRJ) passed its PREA audit on the first review. Newton also discussed his experiences as a certified PREA auditor.

Operational Changes

RRJ spent a couple of years getting ready for its PREA audit. In Newton's experience the single biggest piece of preparing for a PREA audit is educating the staff and taking them through the cultural changes needed to make inmate safety their topmost priority. As policies and processes continued to evolve, staff needed further retraining. PREA diverted training hours away from other priorities.

Adjustments for PREA compliance included the following.

> ➤ Classification used to have a 72-hour window to interview new inmates, who would be held in a pre-classification housing unit. That's no longer acceptable: an agency can't house any inmates together before a risk assessment identifies likely victims or predators. Inmates need to be placed where they say they can feel safe. In RRJ, a multidisciplinary team makes a housing determination for indicated inmates prior to their introduction into general housing. There still is no model risk assessment available for agencies to use. Individuals identified as likely predators or victims as well as LBGTI inmates must be reassessed/reclassified within 30 days.

> ➤ Transgender inmates pose their own challenges. The RRJ facility typically houses around five to eight transgender individuals at a time. All so far have been transwomen (men who have changed or are changing to a physical identity as women), and they have been in the jail at various points in their physical transition to female. The jail now asks these inmates a series of questions as they enter the facility, and a multidisciplinary team meets with them. Most important is the inmate's view of where she thinks she'll be safe. A transwoman who still had a penis was placed in a women's housing unit. It was unexpected and unsettling at first, but it worked.

> ➤ RRJ delivers all of its educational content on PREA to inmates on arrival instead of providing an overview on arrival and further information within 30 days. When PREA education was launched, classification staff went around to every unit to deliver training to

inmates who were already in the jail. Inmates signed a roster to document that they attended the training, saw the video, received reading material, got information on how to report a violation, etc.

➢ Employee background checks are worthwhile. Some staff members have been with the agency for 25 years, and no background investigations had been done for all that time.

➢ Installing more cameras addressed issues with blind spots.

➢ It's important to have an anonymous method for staff to report allegations to avoid the possibility of retaliation. Allegations from staff in RRJ can be submitted online and go straight to investigators.

➢ A sexual abuse investigation debrief must be held within 30 days of the alleged incident, unless the allegation is determined to be unfounded. If an agency has a founded allegation, Newton recommended assembling the staff members to run through the process for the first time before the formal debrief. The debriefing should include all staff members who have any involvement in the agency's PREA response. An incident debrief in RRJ did not include maintenance staff who were responsible for security cameras. The debrief revealed issues with the positioning of cameras that were later addressed.

➢ The agency needed a mechanism for proving its efforts to prevent retaliation against inmate perpetrators and victims for at least 90 days after an allegation. RRJ holds meetings between the inmate and the investigator and documents the fact that they met. Other agencies are coordinating this via the facility's PREA coordinator or an investigator.

➢ RRJ needed to establish a process to tell the inmate what the results of investigation were, even after the inmate has been released from custody.

➢ A coordinated PREA response plan has been useful for RRJ. The plan is a simple matrix that identifies who is responsible for what actions. The staffing plan and staffing analysis posed the biggest challenge to incorporate information on factors such as camera locations, data on previous incidents, and the facility's physical plant. It's more than a budget analysis of how many people the agency can afford to have. There is no template to follow.

Audits and Auditors

Auditors are independent, and each auditor has his or her own focus. Each agency hires its own auditor from a list of DOJ-approved providers. RRJ picked someone who had long experience as an ACA accreditation auditor. The process begins with the agency providing information to the auditor a month in advance of the on-site audit. This can raise questions that can be addressed before the visit.

As an auditor, Newton is finding it takes 30 to 40 hours for document review before the 2-day site visit. Larger facilities may require another on-site day. Report writing can take an additional week. Only the lead auditor needs to have DOJ audit certification.

Agencies can prepare for the audit by conducting practice interviews with staff so they know what the auditor will ask. Audit questions are available from the PREA Resource Center. Newton said that some of the best conversations during the audits he's conducted were with inmates. Inmates did not see the interviews as an opportunity to lodge complaints against the staff.

Auditors are not there to play "gotcha." They evaluate the jail on each element of a standard and decide whether the jail is substantially compliant. The outcome is either that the jail meets the PREA standards 100% or it doesn't. Jail leadership can talk with their auditor about how to become compliant. Jail officials should know the difference between a requirement for compliance and a recommendation. An auditor can't ask or require the jail to install cameras; they can only make the recommendation.

Challenges

In RRJ's case, some PREA issues were related to staffing analysis. The agency's staffing analysis document was the last thing they finished.

Newton was originally concerned that PREA compliance would create huge costs for the agency, but this hasn't been the case. Cameras and physical plant investments cost money, but the most significant expense has been staff training and education and PREA's effect on training priorities. RRJ personnel trained local police on PREA investigation procedures, using training material from the PREA Resource Center. Six investigators have been trained. Community support has been strong.

It was initially thought that finding a community partner to receive allegation reports would be difficult or that the agencies would not know what they were getting into. A rape crisis center is providing this service at no charge. Fears of multiple complaints being handled by community advocates turned out to be unfounded.

The RRJ campus has a main jail and a community corrections center. Both were audited under the PREA jail audit instrument. For future audits, only the jail will be audited under the jail standards.

Initially the standards called for facilities with 500 beds or more to have a full-time PREA coordinator. That standard was changed. RRJ facilities have a PREA coordinator and a PREA compliance manager.

Discussion

- ➢ Most U.S. jails are technically out of compliance with PREA, because so few have undergone and passed their first audit. Newton made certain to get RRJ in compliance by the August 2014 deadline in order to renew a contract to house federal inmates. Other agencies may be at risk of losing revenue if the Federal Bureau of Prisons, ICE, and other federal agencies stop using their beds. States that are not in compliance with PREA also are subject to losing 5% of federal grant money. Currently, 41 states are not in compliance but have stated to DOJ that they intend to be.

- ➢ In Newton's opinion, agencies that refuse to comply with PREA eventually will be sued, and the claimants will have an advantage in showing deliberate indifference. Jails that do well in an audit—even if they don't achieve 100% compliance—will be in a stronger position in litigation. Now that PREA is law, the debate is over, but corrections professionals still should advocate for some changes in the PREA standards.

PART 2. SURVIVING THE PREA AUDIT

Presenter: Marilyn Chandler Ford, Director, Volusia County Corrections, Daytona Beach, Florida

Volusia County has a county-run jail, and its personnel have been implementing PREA requirements since 2008. Chandler Ford framed the county's audit preparations by establishing timelines for the overall process: hiring the auditor, receiving the audit report, and remediation.

County purchasing requirements meant that the jail had to get bids from auditors. Incoming bids differed in whether they included working with the jail on remediation efforts and whether certain costs were included in the price or would be compensated by the jail separately. A spreadsheet was helpful for comparing which costs—such as transportation—were included in the base price.

All the jail's operational teams provided extensive documentation that was compiled on a flash drive and sent to the auditor.

Generally, Chandler Ford found that the auditor accurately identified the items that Volusia County had not been able to address as well as they hoped. She had been prepared to argue on behalf of the agency's efforts, but she had no major disagreements with the auditor's findings.

The written findings could have been clearer on what was considered a violation of the standards as opposed to a recommendation for improvement. The initial audit report did not identify the exact standards that were met or not met. These points were clarified in the exit interview and in follow-up communications with the auditor.

The formal PREA audit process includes a 180-day period for corrective action. Auditors can work with agencies to verify their remedial action. Chandler Ford commented that remediation will take longer than the agency expects.

The jail is continuing to address issues raised, such as the following.

> The auditor found that despite the training provided to staff, some of the principles had not been internalized. One of the jail's contract providers did very poorly answering questions, though the company had done its own training, too. At the same time, some staff members feel over-trained on PREA. Volusia County is launching regular, survey-based quizzes on PREA and other topics and will continue to cover aspects of PREA in roll call training.

> Blind spots are difficult to address in the jail's linear-style building; installing enough cameras would be too expensive. Volusia County is adding more mirrors in the jail and will increase staff rounds in housing units. It will also add the use of a proximity device to electronically register security rounds by staff in general population blocks.

> The jail added a second officer in the control room for part of the day to accommodate the additional number of cameras that need monitoring.

> ➢ Dormitories are being replaced. The auditor said the jail did not provide adequate information on the design of the buildings to show their PREA readiness.

> ➢ The jail now has two PREA compliance managers overseeing its two facilities. The additional manager is knowledgeable and came from the case management classification area.

> ➢ A large amount of PREA-relevant policy and procedure is being moved to other policies. An example is in background checks at hiring. For audit purposes, the topics will continue to be mapped in an agency PREA master plan that covers every standard.

Chandler Ford's overall experience with the audit has been positive. She can congratulate her staff on their achievements, and the county is pleased with the jail's performance.

The audit showed:

> ➢ Staff members who operate the jail accept PREA and understand the principles of zero tolerance.

> ➢ Inmates understand that the jail practices zero tolerance and say they feel safe.

> ➢ The jail follows best practices and operates a safe and humane facility. There are a few areas still to be strengthened.

Budget implications of PREA are coming into better focus. From an initial estimate of about $250,000 to remediate, the current price tag is closer to $100,000, including the PREA coordinator position. Mirrors and cameras added up to around $80,000.

– – –

PROGRAM SESSION:
HEALTH CARE REFORM + INMATE MEDICAL CARE = REDUCED COSTS?

PART 1. AFFORDABLE CARE ACT: CONTINUITY OF CARE

Presenter: Richelle Arhalt, Administrator, Dane County Sheriff's Office, Madison, Wisconsin

The Affordable Care Act (ACA) is an element in how the Dane County jail is leveraging medical and mental health care partnerships in the community. Its medical care contract is $4.4 million per year.

A hospital utilization management plan ensures inmates are getting appropriate treatment while minimizing out-of-facility stays. The jail is responsible for only those outside medical care costs that the inmate is unable to pay. The jail rarely sees medical bills for inmates' hospital care. As a result, Dane County is less likely than other jails to see an immediate cost savings from Medicaid expansion under the ACA.

Discharge planning helps bridge the gap to ensure continuity of care and medication and is especially important with inmates who have mental illnesses. A rise in chronicity of conditions means that more inmates are leaving the jail facility with health issues. Benefits for inmates who are already on Medicaid terminate when they enter the facility and must be restarted when they leave.

It's easiest to make arrangements for sentenced inmates who have a known release date. Assisting other inmates is more challenging and will be a future focus of the jail. The jail's allies include the county's human services re-entry coordinator, Americorps, the county public health agency, various community and faith-based groups, and the Public Defender's Office. The jail conducts jail tours for providers to help them understand jail operations and issues with the jail population.

The first step in working with inmates on community care is identifying what benefits inmates will qualify for after release. Inmates usually fill out paper forms because Internet connectivity is difficult in the jail's buildings. They often need help completing lengthy forms. They can get help from the re-entry coordinator, an Americorps staff person, or a volunteer. No jail staff members are currently assigned to help with this paperwork. A task analysis is under way to see if the work can be redistributed.

It's too early at this point to measure the results of linking inmates with Medicaid-covered care in the community. The jail will examine its data to review the benefits to the jail of getting inmates connected with community services, in terms of real dollars and reductions in recidivism.

Discussion

➢ A meeting participant from Maryland described ways Medicaid expansion is saving the county money on inmate care costs. Costs for inmates who are hospitalized for 23 hours or more are paid by Medicaid instead of being the jail's responsibility. Care for inmates who are hospitalized for dialysis is now covered. Medicaid also pays for medications once inmates are released. Inmates who arrive at the jail with an injury are admitted to the jail first and then transferred to the hospital for medical care so their care will be covered by Medicaid.

➤ Counties in Florida have organized to negotiate below-Medicaid rates for hospital services for jail inmates. The Florida Sheriffs' Association was involved.

PART 2. AFFORDABLE CARE ACT: INNOVATIVE APPROACHES

Presenter: Raul Benasco, Jail Chief, Bexar County Sheriff's Office, San Antonio, Texas

Bexar County's approach to inmate/ex-inmate medical and mental health care aims to allocate community resources based on assessed risks and needs. Agencies working with an overlapping clientele share protocols and infrastructure. Inmate medical care in Bexar County is provided in-house, with special services obtained through a partnership with the university medical school system, which is the county's medical health provider. The partnership also provides the jail access to the county's automated medical records system. The jail is equipped to provide dialysis and other services to reduce costs for hospital services. In Texas, Medicaid benefits are suspended, not terminated, when detainees enter the jail.

The Haven for Hope community center is a key asset in connecting former inmates with wellness services. These services reduce recidivism, especially among women who may be pregnant and/or addicted. Many inmates have had no medical care for years before arriving at the jail.

All jail classification officers have tablet computers. Assessment information is dropped straight into the facility's data system without a paper interface. Shared data promotes system-wide efficiencies and can be particularly helpful in the development of grant applications.

The jail is focusing on several aspects of care and community connectedness.

➤ It is educating county commissioners and the public about the ACA and how Medicaid expansion will affect jail costs. No one should rush to cut the jail's medical care budget.

➤ It is educating inmates, their families, and the jail's outside partners on how to reactivate former inmates' Medicaid benefits and benefits due to military veterans. Inmates' status as adjudicated or pre-adjudicated is relevant.

➤ It is establishing health care connections at reentry. Continuity of care is essential. Video visitation is helping. Inmates are released with 90-day release plans. Medicaid enrollment and re-enrollment takes staff time and funds, plus supportive technology. An assessment center where ex-inmates can get services is located near the jail, which makes it more likely that they will get the assistance they need and will not return to jail custody.

➤ It is establishing processes for cost recovery. The jail is not yet hitting its targets.

> ➤ It is establishing inpatient vs. outpatient status of inmates receiving hospital care and their eligibility for Medicaid coverage. A patient is not considered the jail's inmate until a proxy booking is conducted.

> ➤ It is considering whether to focus on enrolling individual inmates in Medicaid or, instead, to attempt to enroll most of the inmate population. A strong JMS system will be necessary to support this work so double data entry can be avoided for information already in the medical records.

> ➤ It is conducting behavioral health assessments 24/7—when inmates arrive at the jail, while they are in the jail, and prior to release. This information will enable an evaluation of the benefits of the mental health services that are being delivered. Information is shared with the pretrial supervision agency.

Improved access to behavioral health care, including substance abuse treatment, has reduced re-arrest rates by up to 33%. The county is saving $5,000 to $10,000 per person who is treated. Average medical cost savings per person are around $2,500, and those who receive treatment are earning an average of $2,000 in increased income.

PART 3. CURBING THE RISING COST OF HEALTHCARE

Presenter: Mark Bolton, Director, Louisville Metro Department of Corrections, Louisville, Kentucky

Mark Bolton commented that the jail isn't a triage clinic or a hospital, but it sometimes feels that way. The Louisville Metro Department of Corrections (LMDC) recently began working with a new medical care provider to get the right care providers in the right place at the right time. The jail spends $9 million per year on health care, representing 17% of the jail's budget. Some high-priced services, such as dialysis, are provided by the state prison system. Medical team members are at the jail's daily management briefings to discuss high-risk inmates, detoxing inmates, any co-occurring issues, housing locations, and other challenges.

Major health care concerns in the jail arise in connection with detoxing inmates, inmates with mental illness, and the substance abuse crisis.

> ➤ Inmates in detox make up about 4% of the population, or about 50 per day. Of this number, 70% to 80% are coming off of heroin, and 8% to 10% are detoxing from alcohol. In 2012, Louisville was surprised by a jump in heroin use and a spike in inmates who were addicted or detoxing from heroin. After an inmate died in custody, Bolton was able to explain the situation and the jail's response on local television. Since then, the jail has hired a new medical services provider and added a new detox nurse and protocols. A local open-entry community detox center helped the jail to launch a community model, peer-assisted detox program in the jail that uses inmates in recovery as detox monitors for newer inmates. They primarily serve as extra eyes and ears, with oversight from medical staff, and they help keep detoxing inmates hydrated. An on-call detox nurse works closely with the inmates.

The Enough Is Enough model was piloted first with women and then expanded into a men's section as well. The jail has had no detox deaths since the program started.

➢ Mental health care populations have been increasing as state-run psychiatric beds are being lost. Medications make up a sizeable piece of the medical care budget. LMDC has been able to reduce the amount of psychotropic medications being prescribed over the past few years and is providing more inmate counseling, but costs are still very high.

➢ The war on drugs is closely tied to jail operations. Heroin overdose deaths jumped from 3% of overdose deaths in Kentucky in 2011 to 32% in 2013. The increase is thought to be linked to new law enforcement efforts to control prescription drug abuse. Charges of possession and dealing quadrupled from 2011 to 2013, with a 550% increase in persons charged with heroin possession and a 648% increase in persons charged with trafficking.

LMDC has been reducing costs while also improving its medical care via a multifaceted action plan to provide security, safety, and stability.

➢ Early detection of substance abuse problems is important. The entire staff is trained on the signs and symptoms of drug addiction. Detainees who are detoxing are being recognized on arrival. Portable breathalyzers are used at intake to screen for intoxication, since not all those who are intoxicated were driving at the time of arrest. Body scanners are helping reduce drug contraband. Conditions such as wounds, severe intoxication, medical fragility, and neurological instability are leading more detainees to be deferred prior to booking.

➢ A dual diagnosis functional workgroup brings together stakeholders who provide services to many of the same clients: homeless services, emergency medical services, the University of Louisville hospital, the prosecutor, and others.

➢ "Kynectors" are (re-)enrolling LMDC inmates in ACA-enabled Medicaid coverage. Inmates' benefits are terminated when they enter Kentucky jails.

➢ Policy compliance and auditing is being increased, and LMDC is working with an independent healthcare contract compliance monitor. Reports are posted online for transparency.

➢ LMDC has been able to reduce medication expenses broadly by establishing a formulary and requiring all physicians to use it. The jail has obtained 340B pricing on medications for HIV and Hepatitis C through its relationship with the University of Louisville hospital.

➢ The medical services provider uses in-house procedures when possible, reducing off-site care.

➢ LMDC is linking its jail management system with electronic medical records for inmates. A medication administration management program has eliminated medication errors.

➢ Medical and mental health care issues are communicated more extensively both within the facility and with local and state government agencies.

– – –

PROGRAM SESSION:
MENTAL HEALTH CARE MODELS THAT WORK

PART 1. RESTORATION OF COMPETENCY PROGRAM

Presenter: Gregory Garland, Deputy Chief, San Bernardino County Sheriff's Department, San Bernardino, California

Like many other detention agencies, the jail in San Bernardino County, California, has housed a number of pretrial inmates with mental illnesses who lack competency to stand trial. They would go to court, be found incompetent and return to the jail, and the jail would find a state hospital bed for them—a process that could take 60 to 120 days.

A local placement option has been the Patton State Hospital, a large forensic mental hospital. It has a campus environment and with perimeter security provided by the state corrections agency. After a stay of several months and stabilization on their medications, inmates were returned to the jail for their court appearance. Those who again decompensated in the jail were sent back to Patton. Some inmates would cycle back and forth for years, especially those held on more serious charges.

Inmates who are unlikely ever to be ready for court are now being moved out of the justice system. To help other inmates become competent for trial, San Bernardino County chose to participate in a 2-year, state grant-funded pilot program. The pilot began in 2011 with 20 mentally ill inmates who were selected by the county's department of behavioral health after an assessment process. The effort was facilitated by Liberty Healthcare Corporation, the jail's mental health care partner.

Inmates were placed in a special housing unit in the jail and assessed weekly or more often by a multidisciplinary team to track progress. Reports were provided back to the judges. About 90% of participants were on psychotropic medications. There was no use of forced medications. Rewards to inmates, such as pizza, helped with compliance. Nurses, psychiatrists, psychologists, social workers, and others were in the unit 24/7 to do whatever was needed to keep the participants functioning, to ensure they understood why they were in jail, and to ensure they understood the court process. Inmates were shown photographs of the judge who would hear their case. By helping the inmates know what to expect, the program helped them cope successfully with their court appearance.

The 2-year pilot program worked with about 300 inmates and achieved a 99% success rate. All but a few inmates were stabilized for court and their cases were adjudicated. Three participants did not complete their court appearance and were returned to the state hospital. Before the pilot, the average length of stay (ALOS) for this population was 765 days. The ALOS for those in the pilot program dropped to 86 days. The range was 14 to 150 days in jail. Neighboring Riverside County has experienced similar results. California is making more grant funding available for the program. San Bernardino seeks to expand its program to 60 beds.

PART 2. MENTAL HEALTH TREATMENT

Presenter: Major Christopher Kneisley, Palm Beach County Sheriff's Office, West Palm Beach, Florida

Mentally ill detainees arrive at the Palm Beach County Jail with a formal written request for services from the arresting officer. Under Florida's Baker Act, individuals are provided involuntary mental health examinations. This process diverts misdemeanants with mental health issues to Baker Act receiving centers, which are designated crisis stabilization units or hospitals. Clients can be held for 72 hours then must be released or a petition filed for involuntary placement in a care facility.

Two judges are assigned to a mental health court. Two counselors collect medical and mental health information from outside providers to support the judges' decisions. Public defenders are usually involved. The jail's mental health staff work well with the court and sometimes assist with assessments.

The jail operates chronic care clinics in both of its facilities. About one-quarter of jail inmates are monitored by mental health staff daily. The jail has four, 27-bed direct supervision units for mental health populations. One pod has long-term mental health housing. The units are operated with one officer per 12 beds, or one officer per shift per unit, plus mental health technicians and others who are not security officers. A psychiatrist is present during the week and on call on weekends. Psychologists can put inmates on watch status, but only the psychiatrist can reduce their watch level. Counselors are available 24/7. Unit staff are trained in crisis intervention techniques including communication skills and de-escalation. They recognize when noncompliant behaviors are mental health-related. Consistent staffing of teams creates better communication between inmates and staff.

A triage team meets daily. It includes medical, mental health, and security staff (a sergeant or an officer). The team reviews all cases, including those on special watch status. Within the units, strict protocols are followed, which limit the discretion given to officers. The security captain and medical staff make decisions.

Discharge planning from the unit coordinates the release of mentally ill inmates to the general population, to the street, or to prison.

PART 3. MENTAL HEALTH MANAGEMENT UNIT

Presenter: Jared Schecter, Sedgwick County Sheriff's Office, Wichita, Kansas

The Sedgwick County jail recently received funding for a Mental Health Management Unit and opened it in 2014. It operates in four direct supervision housing pods, including one unit for women. Inmates are screened by a triage nurse during intake and can be placed in the MHMU after review.

The MHMU is managed differently than other units. Admittance decisions are made by the mental health treatment team and jail management. Inmates get briefed to different expectations. They can leave their cells and are held to the same behavioral standards as general population inmates.

Programming includes medication management, training on coping skills, and education on criminogenic factors. A social worker provides prerelease planning, including linkages with community providers and an appointment the day after release to ensure continuity of medications. Kansas terminates Medicaid benefits when inmates are admitted to the jail. Getting these appointments took 30 days in the past, and many releasees ended up returning to the jail in the interim. The social worker helps get their benefits started or re-started.

Detention officers work closely with mental health professionals. They document inmates' behavior and use crisis intervention skills as needed. Officers rotate onto the unit for 2-week assignments. Because the officer's role is more intensive than in other units, the jail found that doing this job for an entire month was too demanding.

Inmate management is defined by behavioral level.

➢ Inmates at Level 1 may be showing unusual behaviors or experiencing some difficulty functioning but are not suicidal. They are not confined to their cells and can mingle with other inmates in the unit. Their behavior is monitored by unit staff.

➢ Inmates at Level 2 show a decrease in coping skills; they receive three assessments per week and a wellness check every 30 minutes.

➢ Level 3 includes all inmates who are new to the unit and those who are markedly disturbed or considered at potential risk for self-harm. They are confined to their cells under staff observation and are assessed three times per week.

➢ Level 4 inmates are acutely disturbed and/or on suicide watch. They are housed in an area with single cells under very close supervision and are clothed in a suicide smock.

➢ Inmates at Level 5 pose a risk to themselves or others and may be restrained if necessary. Mental health and detention staff may confer on moving these inmates out of jail custody.

Most inmates are discharged from the unit out into the community. At first it was thought that many inmates would eventually transition into general population, but experience has shown that most inmates with mental illnesses function better separately. In general population, too many were challenged by the lack of structure and began to decompensate.

Goals for the unit are changing. Inmates are benefitting from skilled officer management, social interaction on the pod, and the coordinated discharge planning. One indicator of success with MHMU is a 74% decrease in use of force incidents involving inmates with mental illnesses. This is related to a need for fewer cell extractions.

PART 4. MENTAL HEALTH TREATMENT AND COMMUNITY RE-ENTRY

Presenter: Don Pinkard, Jail Commander, Gwinnett County Sheriff's Office, Lawrenceville, Georgia

The Gwinnett County Detention Center operates a 40-bed crisis stabilization unit that includes two dormitory housing units and private cells with glass fronts. The deputy nurse's post has a view of everyone housed in the unit. Inmates are placed there because of current behavior or past history that identifies them as being in or at high risk for a mental health crisis. Patients on suicide precautions and psychiatric observation are admitted to this unit by the clinical staff and are evaluated at least daily until the treatment team has determined the patient is stable enough to be housed in another area.

Two special management units with 30 and 40 beds provide housing for inmates with a diagnosis of severe and persistent mental illness (SPMI). Officers working in these units have training in crisis management. Inmates receive clinical treatment and a variety of adjunctive therapeutic programming, including animal assisted therapy, music therapy, and yoga. To participate, inmates must be medication-compliant and have no behavioral disruptions within the previous 14 days. Every Monday, clinical and security staff meet to discuss the status of people on the unit.

Agency representatives, advocates, attorneys, and program staff meet monthly to match inmates with services on release. There has been great success from getting people into a room to talk together about what to do with a person who needs services. There is still no good answer on how to manage people who can't be kept stabilized on their medications.

The starting point with the community reentry effort was to meet with Georgia Supreme Court judges, solicitors, and the district attorney to get them to understand the seriousness of issues with mentally ill populations in the justice system. Ultimately a judge took action to address the lack of available services. The Sheriff's Office also reached out to probation and parole and the area's faith community, connecting organizations that had not been talking to each other. Progress was slow at first. Then funding was allocated, the United Way came in as a partner, and the commission on homeless also got involved.

Now, the jail's Community Bridge program links inmates with treatment after release. It provides significant assistance to SPMI patients who would have difficulty advocating for services for themselves after release. In 2012, 49 individuals were enrolled in community services, and 42 remain in treatment. In addition, the Gwinnett Re-entry Intervention Program (GRIP) was launched in February 2012 as a partnership with multiple community agencies on re-entry efforts. It connects inmates with assistance in housing, drug/alcohol treatment, job skills training, and other services.

Community partnerships can be built by asking engaging organizations that already work with inmates and/or persons with mental illness. Clients who can pay for services are more appealing to community organizations, or the jail may be able to obtain a grant or find resources that can be reallocated. Finally, patients need to be encouraged to take advantage of available services and comply with treatment plans.

– – –

PROGRAM SESSION:
JAIL LEADER LONGEVITY IN OFFICE

ACHIEVING AND SUSTAINING SUCCESS IN JAIL LEADERSHIP

Facilitator: Patrick Tighe, Director of Detention, St. Lucie County Sheriff's Office, Fort Pierce, Florida

In this session, participants shared their thoughts about the factors that enable jail directors to succeed over the long term in a complex, public safety leadership post.

Skills necessary to the position include political and organizational skills, planning, personal time management, negotiation, complex problem solving, listening, and forecasting. Maintaining a balance between work and personal life is a given, unless the leader is willing to accept the loss of that balance.

Many jail leaders develop skills in areas they did not anticipate, such as jail design and construction oversight.

Balance

Jail leaders must keep the interests of staff and inmates in balance for smooth operation of the facility. It can be like walking a tightrope. If too much weight is given to staff preferences, the culture may change such that use of force increases.

Mission creep is a risk, as the jail's role has expanded over the years into areas such as GED programming, mental health services, and substance abuse treatment.

Oversight

It is essential to watch the jail's statistical indicators and respond to them when needed. Anything could be a clue to a larger issue: erroneous releases, use of force incidents, inmate-on-inmate assaults. Share the numbers with staff, and the numbers will change.

Perspective

Jail leaders need to keep up with new ideas outside their own agency and region. Participating in Large Jail Network meetings and professional associations helps a leader stay open and aware.

Successful jail leaders operate with the personal mission of making their jails better. Leaders don't settle for whatever success they have; they want more. Attending a meeting such as the LJN provides a chance for self-examination and a step back. All of the jails represented at the meeting are doing well because of a commitment to improvement. A leader wants to leave the agency better than when he/she got there.

Credibility, Trust, and Relationship Building

Jail leaders need the ability to gain the trust of others—staff, county commissioners, sheriffs, and community stakeholders and partners. Being connected with the community is essential for getting new approaches explored and implemented.

Being the voice of careful resource utilization develops credibility with local government.

Working effectively with unions is important where personnel are unionized. After working in good faith with union representatives on their priorities, jail leaders can turn to them for help implementing policy changes.

The reality of jail management is what goes on behind the office doors, not in what the media says about the jail.

Jail leaders should develop good relationships with the state's attorney, local judges, and public defenders. One meeting participant gives the public defender office space in the facility.

Many local jurisdictions offer leadership training for personnel in any agency. Participating in these programs is good not only for skills development but also for developing relationships and educating other officials about the jail's role in the community. One participant was able to get an Affordable Care Act navigator assigned to the jail through a connection made at a local leadership training session.

Recognizing the concerns of stakeholders builds loyalty.

➢ One agency sponsors an annual luncheon for 350 clergy volunteers. When county budgets come to a vote, clergy attend the session and sit in the front rows to show support for the jail.

➢ Similarly, it's important to reach out to groups such as the local NAACP chapter, the ACLU, the school board, and the health department.

➢ Support the media by giving them the information they need to do their jobs, and their coverage of jail issues will be more fair and accurate.

➢ Developing contacts with bondsmen can make them assets in recovering inmates after an erroneous release.

➢ Include contracted service providers in the agency's command staff meetings. Their success is your success.

Advocacy and Education

Jail leaders often are catalysts in getting inmate needs met through partnerships. They also advocate for detention as a profession deserving of equal respect as other sheriff's department functions.

Jails are full of personnel dedicated to a mission, and the public seldom knows much about it. Jail leaders can make a difference by helping the media report on what jails do. Share data and information on how many mentally ill inmates the jail houses, what reentry programs are offered, the number of meals served daily, and the jail's hospice care and dog adoption programs.

Open the jail to tour groups of federal, state, and local government officials and other stakeholders.

A Focus on the Long-Term Interests of the Organization

A successful jail leader keeps the best interests of the agency foremost. It's sometimes important to project a sense of selflessness.

Jail leaders can sit in on new recruit interviews and ask the recruits what they think the job involves. This is a way of bringing into the jail personnel who are open to a culture that focuses on the whole person. Instead of "care, custody, and control," one participant looks for potential officers who can appreciate the jail's role as being about "care, craft, and cause." In his view, craft is about being creative for a purpose. The cause of the jail's work is not the mission statement; it's the aim to have all staff going home safe at the end of their shift.

A leader needs to think toward the future when he or she will hand off responsibilities to a successor. One element in the hand-off is transitioning key, trusted relationships both inside and outside the agency.

Perseverance

All larger detention agencies can be expected to go through difficult times and to face tragedies. After a critical incident, the staff and jail leadership need to get together and talk about what happened. The point is not the tragedy itself—it's what the agency does about it. A jail leader will show people in and outside the agency that the agency will continue to improve its operations and turn the situation around. This calls for a type of perpetual optimism. The jail leader and the people he or she relies on need to get up in the morning and keep going.

– – –

OPEN FORUM

"Hot topic" sessions for the meeting are an opportunity for participants to discuss emerging issues. The sessions were coordinated and presented by Mitch Lucas, Charleston County, South Carolina.

BODY CAMERAS

Participants noted no systemic problems in the use of body-worn video cameras. Data storage is becoming less expensive. Federal money may be available for purchasing cameras for on-person use or other purposes.

Major issues with body cameras are batteries going dead when needed, officers not turning on the unit at the appropriate time, and the need for comprehensive policies on recording storage, access, and review by supervisory staff.

Training must be clear. Officers may forget to the turn on the camera when an incident begins. In one location, the union advised that the cameras should be used only when there is a major use of force, leading to confusion among officers.

For evidentiary purposes, the best cameras do not allow file download except through the jail's secure computer network.

Officers in at least one jail have been on duty with a personally owned video camera. This raises policy issues on storage, review, and access, among other aspects, and it should not be allowed.

A court decided that DUI interactions needed to be on video or the case was no good. Taser International is offering body cameras to police that store the recording "in the cloud." A mobile device application is now available that captures video of the device owner's interactions with law enforcement in a traffic stop. The recording can be accessed immediately by the attorney that markets the app.

RESTRICTED HOUSING

Jail professionals are urged to watch what happens with H.R. 4618, the Solitary Confinement and Reform Act of 2014, and to educate their legislators, including its 23 co-sponsors, about the use of restricted housing in jails. The bill has been referred to the U.S. House Judiciary Committee's Subcommittee on Crime, Terrorism, Homeland Security, and Investigations. Advocacy and attention on solitary confinement could follow a similar path as the focus on inmate sexual assault that led to passage of the Prison Rape Elimination Act. The measure reflects concerns expressed by inmate advocacy groups about aspects such as the negative effects on inmates of long-term isolation when used as a disciplinary tool.

Jail inmates are most likely to be housed alone when they are in protective custody or administrative segregation, when they have medical or mental health issues that require separation, or when they are the only juvenile inmate in the jail's custody.

Some jail inmates stay in restricted housing because they continue to violate rules or pose a security risk. Others cycle between general population and special housing as their behavior changes because of mental health issues. Regular reviews by mental health staff are appropriate.

Jail leaders are advised to review and update their policies on step-down from restricted housing under various circumstances. With objective jail classification tools in place, decision-making is easier to do and to document.

SCANNING DRIVERS LICENSES FOR VISITOR REGISTRY

Some jails are scanning driver's licenses as a time-saver for staff assigned to check identities of inmates' visitors. However, about 50% of licenses won't scan, according to a participant. Scanning can also enable checks of the warrant system.

SCHEDULING VISITATION

Participants discussed the pros and cons of scheduling face-to-face inmate visits. It adds work for officers, but families appreciate it. Waiting lines are less likely to form, which is especially helpful when children are present. Some jails are allowing inmates to schedule their visits via kiosk, reducing the burden on staff.

Video visitation is convenient. Family members typically pay for the visit. Communities including Pinellas County offer mobile visitation units; the Pinellas visitation bus returns to the same neighborhood each week and has six visiting stations. The Sheriff's Office pays for the service.

INTERNAL AFFAIRS INVESTIGATOR TRAINING

ILEETA, the International Law Enforcement Educators and Trainers Association Agency, was recommended as a source of training for internal affairs investigators.

PRESERVING THE SECURITY OF SECURITY PLANS

One jail's construction plans recently were found available for sale on eBay. Security breaches of this type can occur even when an agency hires nationally known architects and construction management companies. To reduce exposure, agency staff must know who has access to facility planning documents and how they are shared, both during bidding and when the project is under way.

E-CIGARETTES

Commissary sales of e-cigarettes generate significant revenue. Cigarettes can be a top motivator for good inmate behavior, and allowing the sale of cigarettes can result in less contraband. One e-cigarette is the equivalent of two packs of the usual tobacco version.

However, inmates can take apart the e-cigarettes and use the menthol unit to get high. One control method is to require inmates to return their first cigarette unit before being issued another.

KOSHER KITCHENS

The Greenville County detention facility recently established a way to provide kosher meals at a fraction of the usual cost. A section of the kitchen has been set aside for preparing kosher meals. Foods prepared there are mainly vegetarian, and a small amount of kosher meat is served. All of the kosher kitchen equipment is labeled so it can be kept separate from other items. The work surfaces are covered with plastic wrap. New food trays and cups were purchased and are kept separate from non-kosher serving ware. The kosher meals are delivered and picked up separately.

CONTRACT MONITORS

Most jails represented at the meeting have designated personnel who monitor the jail's larger contracts as part of their assigned duties. County-level contract staff and staff in the sheriff's office often are involved as well. In one agency, a retired undersheriff provides contract monitoring.

Health care contracts are more likely to have a specialized monitor. Professional certifications are available.

NIC offers an annual training program for executive managers in correctional health care.

PART-TIME EMPLOYEES

Jails can find it an advantage to cover some positions with part-time staff. One jail uses retired custody staff for inmate transportation. The retirees are considered civilian employees.

Another jail conducts a summertime academy for college students. They are trained and work for the jail at a significant cost savings in positions such as kitchen work and transport. Overtime is greatly reduced. The program also creates an employment pool for new officers.

ACA detention standards specify that part-time work cannot exceed 30 hours per week. Security officers still require 40 hours of annual training. Part-time schedules mean that some staff are not on-site at convenient times to get the training they need.

IMMIGRATION HOLDS

Many jails are promptly releasing inmates who have an Immigration and Customs Enforcement (ICE) hold instead of holding them on 48- to 72-hour holds for ICE pick-up. These jails consider it adequate to provide notification when an inmate is ready for release. ICE holds are not a warrant and are not signed by a judge. The ACLU has notified some jails that it is monitoring its ICE holds and releases to ensure detainees are not held too long.

To avoid misunderstandings, jail personnel should make it clear to inmates that the jail does not confer with ICE on their cases.

One jail was not accepting the posting of bonds if it appeared an illegal alien might be deported, because of the potential financial impact on the inmate's family.

INSURANCE FOR COMMUNITY SERVICE PARTICIPANTS

Counties are finding it advisable to obtain insurance policies to cover participants in jail-based community service work programs. If participants get hurt on the job, it deters use of the program and incurs costs. The jail in Orange County, Florida, acquired a supplemental insurance policy to cover its program. The policy pays for incidental hospital expenses.

ROTATING DUTY POST ASSIGNMENTS

Rotating detention officers between posts is a common practice. Reasons for rotation are to avoid inappropriate relationships, burnout, and complacency. Rotating staff also can prevent cliques from forming within the officer staff. Rotation cycles range from 30 days to 6 weeks to 90 days to 6 months. Unions may not agree with job rotation policies. Some jails also rotate their supervisory staff on a fixed schedule, such as every 6 months. Certain posts may be excluded from rotation.

Other jails are open to keeping a person in the same assignment for some time, as long as there is attentive supervision. There are benefits to stability in some posts. The supervisor needs to be observant for any issues, including signals of burnout or over-familiarity.

ARTS PROGRAMS

Many jails have programs in the visual, literary, or performing arts. Teachers can be found in area school districts. Volunteers, funding, and grant writing assistance can come from local cultural and arts councils. Inmates participate in poetry slams and perform Christmas carols. One jail has an annual inmate talent show timed in connection with the "March Madness" college basketball playoffs. Inmates in one jail painted a mural in a recreation yard that included security threat group symbols.

FUNDING FOR RELIGIOUS ITEMS

Jails use commissary funds and donations to pay for some less common items for religious observance. Items may be donated by family members via the chaplain. Other jail material can be repurposed. For example, old blankets can be cut down to make prayer rugs.

TRANDSGENDER CORRECTIONAL STAFF

Corrections agencies generally are prepared to accommodate inmate gender issues, and they can frame situations with transgender staff the same way. A jail in Florida has had one staff member transition from male to female. The agency communicated with staff throughout the process. No harassment occurred. Accommodations were needed in areas such as restroom and locker room access. Adaptations were timed to coincide with the officer getting her new driver's license. The officer has a non-contact post to avoid any pat search objections from women inmates who knew her as a male. She is eligible to work overtime if needed on a female unit. The administration reserves the right to assign the officer wherever it decides, and the officer will accommodate the administration's decisions.

In another jail, a transgender officer applicant was almost turned down, until the jail administrator pointed out the parallels with black and women officers who were not always welcomed into jails a few decades ago.

SUBOXONE

Suboxone is a drug used for treating dependency on opioids such as oxycodone and hydrocodone. Inmates are arriving in jail dependent on Suboxone. It is dispensed as "melt-aways" that dissolve on the tongue. For the first 30 minutes after taking it, the patient is typically too high to function normally in a housing unit. Jails are taking inmates to a community clinic to take the medication.

Jail staff also may be prescribed this medication. One jail had an officer who was injured in a motorcycle accident and was later determined to be unfit for duty in connection with his medication needs.

– – –

PROFESSIONAL ASSOCIATION UPDATES

AMERICAN CORRECTIONAL ASSOCIATION

Presenter: Ben Shelor, Deputy Director of Standards and Accreditation, American Correctional Association, Alexandria, Virginia

Ben Shelor was welcomed to his first LJN meeting. He noted that 141 U.S. jails, or about 5%, have received ACA accreditation. Most are fully accredited on ACA's Standards for Adult Local Detention Facilities, and about seven jails have been certified on the ACA Core Jail Standards. That number is rising.

ACA is preparing stand-alone health care standards for jails. The standards committee also has been tasked with developing new standards for facilities designed specifically to hold ICE detainees. Further work is ongoing within the Core Jail Standards. Some issues that had been addressed in one combined standard will be split back out so that if an agency is unable to meet a standard, it will be more narrowly defined.

An ad hoc committee within the Association of State Correctional Administrators (ASCA) will examine issues related to restricted housing and inmates with mental illnesses. Jail professionals will be represented on the committee and are welcome to contact ASCA to contribute their expertise.

ACA also is providing PREA audits. ACA has reformatted the language of the PREA standards to facilitate auditing. They have received preliminary approval from the U.S. Bureau of Justice Assistance and are under DOJ review. Back-to-back ACA and PREA audits will be convenient for agencies because only one tour through the facility will be needed. Persons who are certified to audit prisons can also audit jails, but ACA will not send a person with only a prison background to audit a jail. About 30% to 40% of ACA's PREA auditors have prior jail experience.

AMERICAN JAIL ASSOCIATION

Presenter: Robert Kasabian, Executive Director, AJA

Bob Kasabian said the American Jail Association (AJA) has graduated more than 650 staff from its National Jail Leadership Command Academy. AJA is now designing a new executive leadership development program that should open in 2015.

Legislative issues continue to be a focus of AJA.

➤ Funding for the Second Chance Act has been reauthorized. In approving the funding, the Senate Judiciary Committee attached an amendment to eliminate some of the penalties related to PREA noncompliance.

➤ A bill has been introduced in the House to reduce the use of solitary confinement. If passed, the measure would establish a national commission to study the issue and develop recommended national standards toward reform. (See also the discussion on p. 28.)

➤ The Federal Communications Commission (FCC) just released a further notice of proposed rulemaking on fees for inmate telephone calls. AJA has engaged with the FCC on the issue of inmate calling systems and has successfully improved their understanding of jail vs. prison operations and aspects such as provider cost recovery, use of inmate telephone system revenue by jails, and intelligence/institutional security. Because jails are so diverse in size and geography, AJA has advocated for alternatives to a single rate. The FCC may call for the elimination of site commissions and ancillary fees. FCC attorney opinions differ on whether the FCC has jurisdiction to set intrastate rates. Agencies may wish to share information more widely on how they use the revenues they gain from their inmate phone systems. Participants discussed how state and national associations of counties are another channel for jails to educate and alert their county officials to the operational and budgetary implications of the FCC's actions.

NATIONAL SHERIFFS' ASSOCIATION

Presenter: Tim Albin, Undersheriff, Tulsa County Sheriff's Office, Tulsa, Oklahoma

Tim Albin noted that the National Sheriffs' Association (NSA) is a valuable source of expertise on a range of public safety issues, though not all sheriffs operate a detention facility. He encouraged meeting participants to join the association. Inmate telephones and solitary confinement are among the issues that will be addressed at the NSA's annual conference in January 2015. NSA also responds to issues raised by advocacy groups, and it offers staff training programs.

Albin returned to jail operations in Tulsa after the county's privatized jail facility was reopened under public management in 2005. He turned to NSA for assistance catching up with 6 years' worth of changes in law and professional practice. NSA and NIC were critical in helping Albin manage the transition successfully.

The professional contacts and learning opportunities that are made available through organizations such as NSA are extremely valuable. Albin commented that it's impossible to put a price tag on a lawsuit that is never filed.

– – –

LARGE JAIL NETWORK BUSINESS

FUTURE MEETING TOPICS

The next meeting of the Large Jail Network is scheduled to be held on March 22-24, 2015, at the National Corrections Academy in Aurora, Colorado.

Meeting participants selected the following topics for the meeting:

- ➢ Veterans in jail
- ➢ Restricted housing
- ➢ Using data/metrics in jail management
- ➢ Reentry and community partnerships
- ➢ Workforce diversity
- ➢ Succession planning/leadership development.

Appendix A

**Large Jail Network
September 2014 Final Meeting Agenda**

LARGE JAIL NETWORK MEETING

September 28-30, 2014 National Corrections Academy Aurora, CO

Agenda

Sunday, September 28

6:00 p.m.   Opening Session... Mike Jackson
                                                    NIC Correctional Program Specialist

7:30 p.m.   Orientation for New Members

8:00 p.m.   ADJOURN

Monday, September 29

8:00 a.m.   Legal Issues.. Carrie Hill

11:30 a.m.   Association Updates..NSA, ACA & AJA

12:00 noon   LUNCH

1:00 p.m.   Sovereign Citizens & Domestic Terror Groups....................................... Steve Cope
                                                    BOP Counterterrorism Unit
                                                    Jeff Woodworth
                            National Joint Terrorism Task Force – BOP Rep.

3:00 p.m.   Open Forum: Hot Topics .... Mitch Lucas
                                                    Charleston County, SC

5:00 p.m.   ADJOURN

Tuesday, September 30

8:00 a.m. PREA — Lessons Learned from Audits ....Jeff Newton
Riverside Regional Jail, VA
Marilyn Chandler-Ford
Volusia County, FL

10:00 a.m. Health Care Reform + Inmate Medical Care = Reduced Costs? ....
Richelle Anhalt
Dane County, WI
Raul Benasco
Bexar County, TX
Mark Bolton
Louisville Metro, KY

12:00 noon LUNCH

1:00 p.m. Mental Health Models That Work .... Gregory Garland
Essex County, MA
Shayne Grannum
Elias Diggins
Denver, CO

3:00 p.m. Longevity in Office .... Pat Tighe
St. Lucie County, FL

4:30 p.m. Future Meeting Topics .... Mike Jackson
NIC

5:00 p.m. ADJOURN

Appendix B

Large Jail Network
September 2014 Participant List

Agency/Organization	First Name	Last Name	Job Title
Arapahoe County Sheriff's Office	Jared	Rowlison	Captain
Arapahoe County Sheriff's Office	Vincent	Line	Bureau Chief
Bexar County Sheriff's Office	Raul	Banasco	Jail Administrator
Brazos County Sheriff's Office	Wayne	Dicky	Jail Administrator
Brevard County Sheriff's Office	Darrell	Hibbs	Major
Broward Sheriff's Office	Gary	Palmer	Executive Director/Colonel
Charleston County Sheriff's Office	Willis	Beatty	Chief Deputy
Charleston County Sheriff's Office	Mitch	Lucas	Assistant Sheriff
Clayton County Sheriff's Office	Robert	Sowell	Jail Administrator
Cobb County Sheriff's Office	Donald	Bartlett	Detention Facilities Director
Dane County Sheriff's Office	Richelle	Anhalt	Captain/Jail Administrator
Davidson County Sheriff's Office	Tony	Wilkes	Chief of Corrections
Denver Sheriff Department	Elias	Diggins	Acting Sheriff
Douglas County Dept. of Corrections	Mark	Foxall	Director
Essex County Correctional Facility	Michael	Frost	Assistant Superintendent
Franklin County Sheriff's Office	Chad	Thompson	Major
Franklin County Sheriff's Office	Geoff	Stobart	Chief Deputy
Fulton County Sheriff's Office	Mark	Adger	Cheif Jailer
Greenville County Detention Center	Marshall	Stowers	Captain
Gwinnett County Sheriff's Office	Don	Pinkard	Jail Administrator/Colonel
Hampton Roads Regional Jail	Taunya	Hatchett	Chief of Security
Hennepin County Corrections	Thomas	Merkel	Director
Henrico County Sheriff's Office	Michael	Wade	Sheriff
Jacksonville Sheriff's Office	Tara	Wildes	Director, Dept. of Corrections
Jefferson County Sheriff's Office	Ron	Eddings	Corrections Administrator
Kent County Sheriff Department	Mark	Neumen	Jail Administrator
King County	William	Hayes	Interim Director
Lake County Sheriff	Mark	Purevich	Jail Administrator
Las Vegas Metropolitan Police Dept.	Richard	Forbus	Corrections Captain
Limestone County Sheriff's Office	Dennis D	Wilson	Sheriff
Los Angeles Co. SO	Eric	Parra	Chief
Louisville Metro Government	Mark	Bolton	Director
Lubbock County Sheriff's Office	Cody	Scott	Chief Deputy
Madison County Sheriff's Office	Steve	Morrison	Chief Deputy
Maricopa County Sheriff's Office	Brian	Lee	Deputy Chief
Maryland Dept. of Pub. Safety and Corr. Services	Ricky	Foxwell	Acting Jail Administrator
Miami Dade DCRS	Daniel	Junior	Interim Assistant Director
Milwaukee County Sheriff's Office	Debra	Burmeister	Major
Multnomah County Sheriff's Office	Daniel	Staton	Sheriff

Multnomah County Sheriff's Office	Michael	Shults	Chief Deputy
Muscogee County Sheriff's Office	Dane	Collins	Jail Commander
Oklahoma County Sheriff	Jack	Herron	Major/Jail Administrator
Onondaga County Sheriff's Office	Esteban	Gonzalez	Chief Deputy
Orange County Corrections Dept.	Karen	Cann	Acting Deputy Chief
Orange County Sheriff's Department	Steven	Kea	Assistant Sheriff
Orleans Parish Sheriff's Office	Jerry	Ursin	Chief Deputy
Palm Beach County Sheriff's Office	Christopher	Kneisley	Major
Pierce Co Sheriff's Office	Karen	Daniels	Chief of Corrections
Pinellas County Sheriff's Office	Paul	Halle	Major-Jail Administrator
Plymouth County Sheriff's Dept.	Melvin	Sprague	Assistant Superintendent
Prince George's County	Mary Lou	McDonough	Director
Riverside Regional Jail Authority	Jeffery	Newton	Superintendent
San Bernardino County Sheriff's Dept.	Gregory	Garland	Deputy Chief
San Francisco Sheriff's Department	Matthew	Freeman	Chief Deputy
Sedgwick County Sheriff's Office	Jared	Schechter	Captain
Seminole County Sheriff's Office	Dennis	Lemma	Chief Deputy
St. Lucie County Sheriff's Office	Patrick	Tighe	Director
St. Louis County Government	Herbert	Bernsen	Director
Travis County Sheriff's Office	Wes	Priddy	Captain
Volusia County Division of Corrections	Marilyn	Chandler Ford	Corrections Director
Washoe County Sheriff's Office	Russell	Pedersen	Assistant Sheriff
Winnebago County Sheriff's Dept.	Andrea	Tack	Jail Superintendent

Appendix C

Index of Past LJN Meeting Topics

LARGE JAIL NETWORK MEETING TOPICS
JUNE 1990 – SEPTEMBER 2014

1990	June	System Approaches to Jail Crowding and Population Management
1991	January	Crowding Strategies and the Impact of Court Decisions
	July	Managing Jail Litigation Linking Jail and Community Programs
1992	January	Fair Labor Standards Act Writing and Negotiating Contracts
	July	Americans With Disabilities Act
1993	January	Blood-Borne and Airborne Pathogens Health Care Costs in Jails
	July	Privatization Programs for Women Offenders
1994	January	Public Policy and Intergovernmental Dimensions of the Role of Jails, Professional Associations in Corrections: Their Influence on National Perspectives of the Role of Jails
	July	Using Data and the Resources of the Bureau of Justice Statistics Developing Resources to Provide Inmate Programs
1995	January	Gangs, Jails and Criminal Justice
	July	Trends in Employee Relations Sexual Harassment
1996	January	The Dilemma of In-Custody Deaths The Crime Bill and Its Impact on Jails
	July	Juveniles in Adult Jails
1997	January	Meeting the Competition of Privatization
	July	21st Century Technology and its Application to Local Jail Information and Operational Needs.
1998	January	The Future of Our Workforce: Pre-employment Testing, Recruiting, Hiring, Training and Evaluating 'New Age' Employees {Generation X} Legal Issues Update — Update of PLRA {Prison Litigation Reform Act}
	July	Taking A Proactive Approach to the Prevention of Employee Lawsuits.
1999	January	Post-Traumatic Stress Syndrome and Critical Incidents: Preparation, Response, and Review Legal Issues Update
	July	Improving Opportunities for Successful Recruitment, Selection, and Retention of Staff.
2000	January	Criminal Justice System Coordination and Cooperation: How the Jail Benefits and the System Is Improved. Legal Issues Update.
	July	Exploring Issues and Strategies for Marketing, Funding, and Auditing Large Jail Systems.
2001	January	The Use of Data for Planning, Decision Making, and Measuring Outcomes.

LARGE JAIL NETWORK MEETING TOPICS
JUNE 1990 – SEPTEMBER 2014

	July	Understanding and Using the Data & Resources of the Bureau of Justice Statistics Staff Issues in Large Jails: Staff Utilization, Relationships, Conduct & Misconduct
2002	January	The Future of Jails, Corrections and Criminal Justice Legal Issues Update
	July	Inmate Medical Care Cost Containment Succession Planning for Future Jail Leaders
2003	January	Addressing the Future of Jail Legislation, Resources and Improving Funding Legislation, Resources and Funding: A Perspective from our Professional Associations The Role and Use of Professional Standards and Internal Affairs Large Jail Network Listserv and Web Technology Legal Issues Update - Health Insurance Portability and Accountability Act of 1996 (HIPAA), Admission Screening
	July	Defining the Future & Exploring Organizational Strategies Impact of Jail Population Changes on Jail Management Jail Standards & Accreditation Use of Technology for Jail Administration & Operation
2004	February	Emergency Preparedness: Planning and Implementation Contagious Disease Identification and Prevention Legal Issues Update - Inmate Medical Confidentiality, Involuntary Mental Health Treatment, Contract Provider Litigation, Arrestee Clothing Searches
	July	Effectively Managing Inmate Gangs in Jails Identifying Problems/Managing Inmate Mental Health
2005	January	Preparing Leaders in Corrections for the Future – NIC's Core Competency Project Training as a Strategic Management Tool Inmate Mental Health: Legal Issues, Management, Diversion Justice and the Revolving Door and Corrections Into the Next Decade
	July	Examining Federal and Local Benefits for Jail Detainees Ethics in the Administration of the Jail Human Resource Issues: Employee Recognition, Attendance, Restricted Duty
2006	January	Implementing PREA: The BJS Report Statistical Analysis: Crowding, Life Safety, Managing Staff Succession Planning The Question of TASERS Legal Issues Update
	July	Diagnosing, Analyzing and Improving the Jails Organizational Culture Planning for Catastrophes and Other Crises Prison Rape Elimination Act (PREA) and Jails Criminal Registration Unit: Hillsborough County, FL

LARGE JAIL NETWORK MEETING TOPICS
JUNE 1990 – SEPTEMBER 2014

2007	January	15th Anniversary Meeting Large Jail Systems Assessment Research Project Changing Organizational Culture Improving Collaboration Between Jails and Mental Health Systems Legal Issues Update
	September	Jail Inmate Re-Entry Programs: Public, Private, Non-Profit Involvement Jail Inmate Re-Entry Issues on a County Level Responding to Women Offenders in Large Jails Excited Delirium: A Problem to be Eliminated or Managed Recruiting, Hiring and Retention of Staff
2008	March	Immigration and Customs Enforcement 287(g) Program Contract Services Media Relations Workforce Development Legal Issues Update
	September	Faith Based Programs Human Resource Management Emerging Technologies Proactive Discipline
2009	March	Illegal Alien Programs Transgender, Lesbian, Gay, and Intersex Inmates Proactive Discipline Part 2 PREA Update Legal Issues Update
	September	PREA Commission Presentation Legislative Updates Successful Pre-Trial and Criminal Justice System Collaborations USDOJ - ADA, CRIPA, LEP Presentation Middle Management Training Programs
2010	March	The Trend of Medical Issues in the Future Creating a Culture of Leadership Creating Efficiencies in the Booking Area R.I.S.E. Program (Henrico County, VA) Coping Skills with and for Staff in Fiscally Tight Times Legal Updates with Bill Collins
	September	ACA Core Jail Standards Comstat Approaches to Accountability and Leadership Battling Complacency in Line Staff and 1st Line Supervisors Return to Work/Terminating the Legitimately Ill Employee Addressing Staff Inmate Fraternization

LARGE JAIL NETWORK MEETING TOPICS
JUNE 1990 – SEPTEMBER 2014

2011	March	Legal Updates Jail Suicide Update PREA Effective Use of Data with Policy Makers
	September	Recovering Jails Staff Issues – Applicants, Discipline and Rumor Control Technology Updates Dealing with FMLA Abuses Prescription Drug Epidemic and the Impact on Jails
2012	March	Legal Issues Update Technology Update Inmate Behavior Management Regulatory Investigations Affecting Jails
	September	Media Relations Civilianization and Use of Volunteers Outsourcing: Pro and Con Mental Health Care in Jails Reentry from Jail
2013	March	No meeting
	September	Affordable Care Act From Corrections Fatigue to Fulfillment PREA Resource Center Legal Issues Update
2014	March	Intelligence Led Policing and Jails Segregation of Inmates for Medical and Mental Health Care Facility Culture and Misconduct Crisis Intervention Training Counterfeiting and Jails Staff Wellness
	September	Legal Issues Update Domestic Threats: Domestic Terrorists and Sovereign Citizens PREA: Audit Lessons Affordable Care Act / Medicaid Mental Health Care Models Jail Leader Longevity in Office